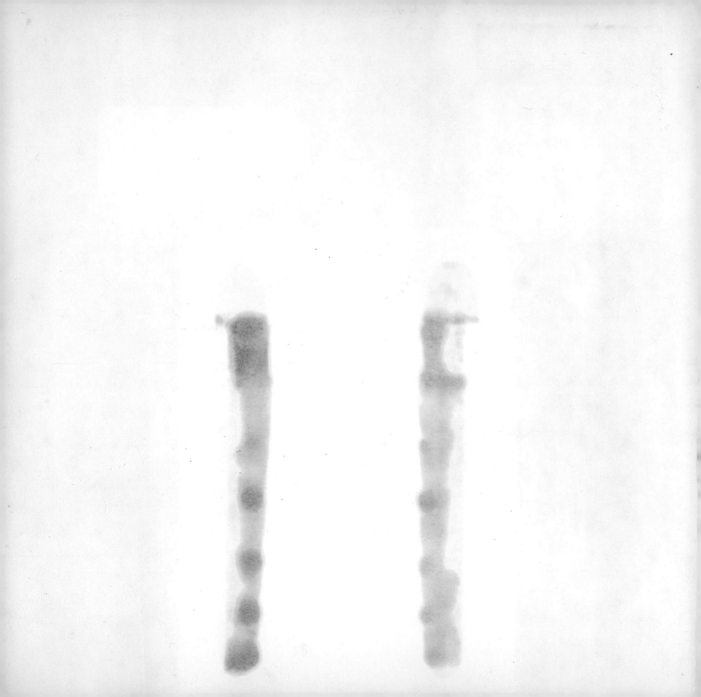

You will need

one large darning needle

a nice selection of
left-over yarn

some scissors

felt scraps

a spool of thread

a thumb tack

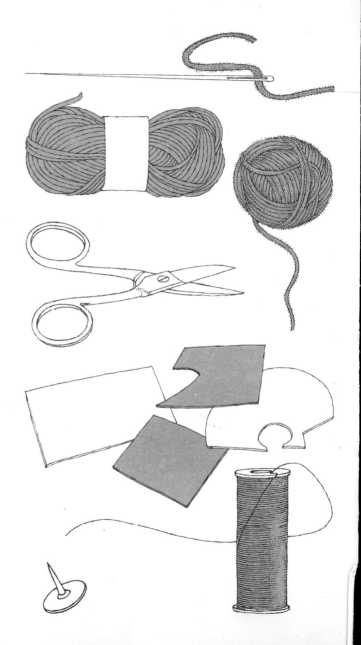

Wool Toys

Written and illustrated by Elsie Wrigley

FREDERICK WARNE · NEW YORK · LONDON

First published by Frederick Warne (Publishers) Ltd.
London, England 1977
First United States publication
Frederick Warne & Co., Inc., New York, New York 1978
Printed in Great Britain · LCC 77–81970 · ISBN 0–7232–1998–2

tissue paper

one hard-boiled egg, to borrow

glue

plastic containers

a shoe box or a small
cardboard box

some scraps of net

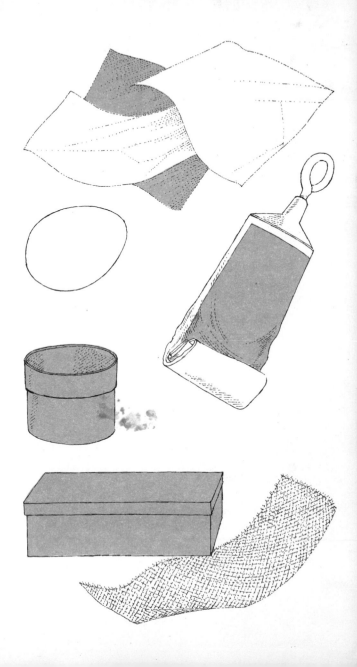

To make a creepy crawly

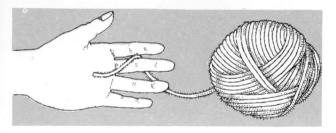

Hold the end of the wool between two fingers.

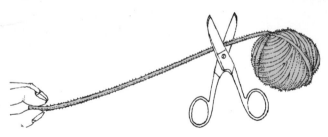

Cut a piece of wool about 8 in. long.

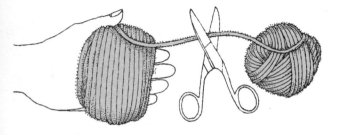

Wind the wool 50 times around four fingers held together. Wind firmly. Cut off the wool.

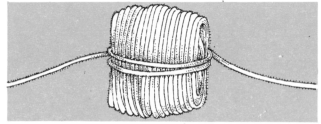

Wind it twice around the center of the wound wool.

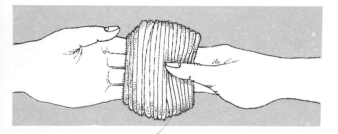

Slip the wound wool carefully off the fingers.

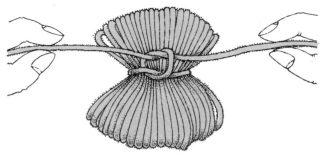

Pull the length of wool tight. Tie it firmly twice.

Make 8 more bundles the same.

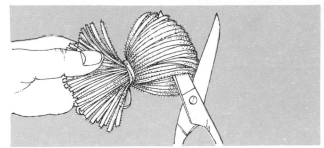

Cut through all the loops of the 10 bundles of wool.

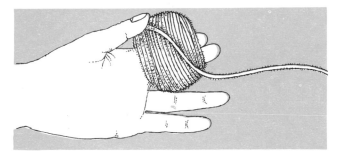

Now wind the wool 40 times around two fingers only.

Flatten the bundle the opposite way.

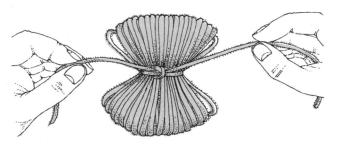

Tie the center tightly as before.

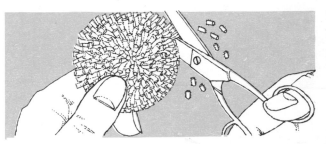

Trim around to a neat circle.

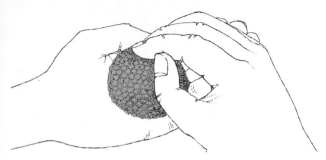

Roll each one in your hands to make a nice ball.

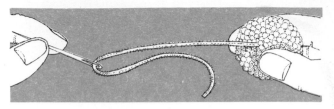

Put the needle into the center of the smallest ball. Push the ball to the end of the wool. Make sure the knot holds tight.

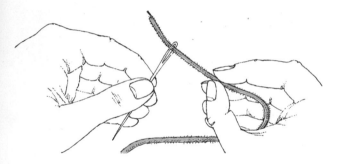

Thread a needle with a big eye with 18 in. of wool.

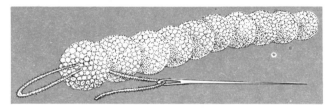

Thread the rest of the balls on to the wool length through their centers so that all the balls touch. Knot securely at the last ball.

Tie a big knot on the end.

Cut three 6 in. lengths of wool.

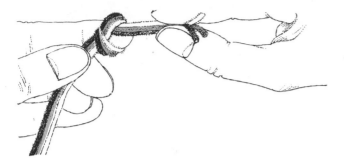

Tie them together at one end.

Before unpinning, tie the other end of the braid.

Pin the knot firmly to a hard surface with a thumb tack.

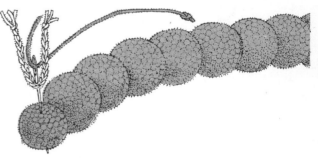

Stitch the center of the braid into the center of the head.

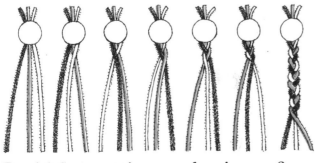

Braid by putting each piece of wool in turn into the center.

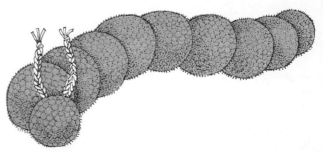

Here is your creepy crawly.

To make rabbits

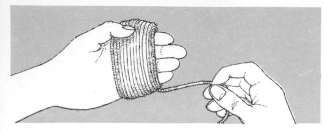

In the same way as before make a large ball on four fingers, winding 60 times for the body.

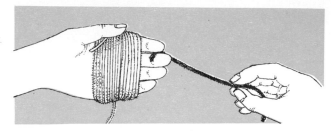

To make a rabbit in two colors begin as usual, winding 20 times, then join in another color, winding 20 times.

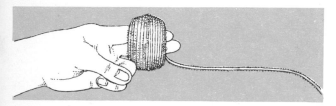

Make a small ball on two fingers, winding 40 times, for the head.

Cut off the second color. Wind 20 times with the first color again.

Make another ball in white on two fingers, winding 30 times for the tail, and trim it even smaller than the head.

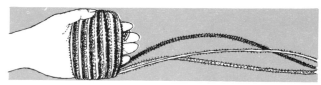

To make speckled color, wind three colors together but only wind 20 times for the body, 13 times for the head.

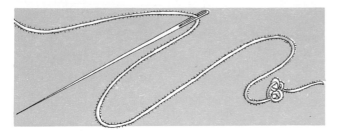

Thread a needle with 12 in. of wool. Tie a big knot on the end.

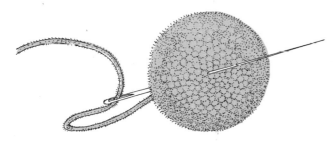

Stitch it firmly into the center of the largest ball.

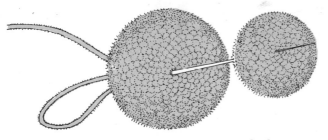

Then up into the center of the medium ball.

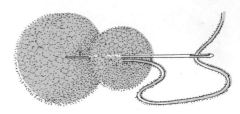

Now back again into the center of the big ball.

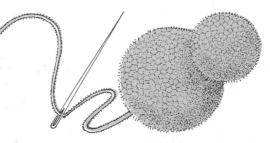

Draw it tight enough to hold the two balls firmly together. Stitch once or twice into the lower end of the big ball.

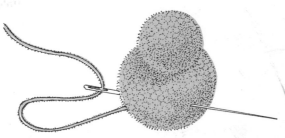

Then bring the needle out at right angles to the head.

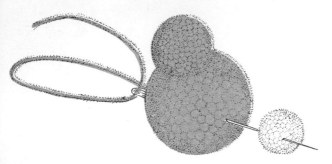

Now through the center of the little white ball.

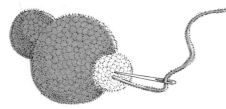

Then back again into the big ball so that the white ball is stitched to the lower end of the body opposite the head, to make a tail. Knot securely.

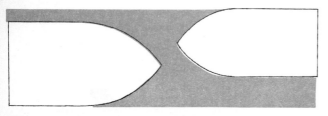

Trace these shapes for ears.

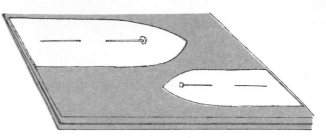

Now, folding the felt once, pin on the patterns.

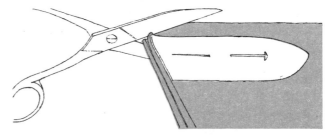

Cut out two large ear shapes, then two small ear shapes.

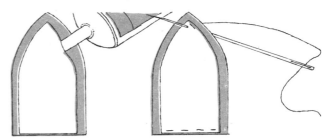

Either glue them together or stitch them at the top corner and bottom edge with thread.

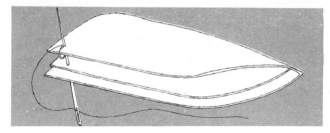

Join together the two bottom corners of each ear.

Make rabbits of different colors, but with white tails.

Stitch them close together into the top of the head.

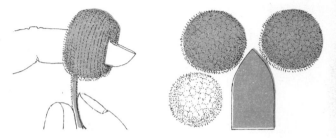

To make baby rabbits use one finger. Wind 20 times for the head and body, 10 times for the tail. Use the small ear shape.

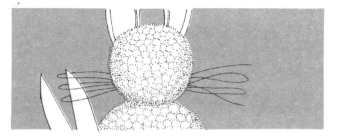

Sew thread through the head for whiskers, making loops on each side. Cut through the loops.

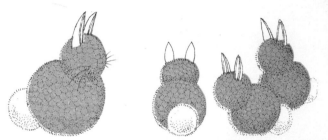

Make a mother and babies.

Rabbit hutch

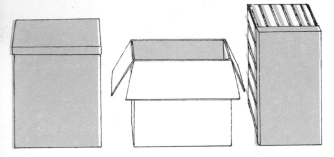

Rabbit hutches can be made from old boxes. Shoe boxes are a good size.

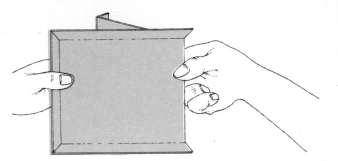

Crease the lid gently. It is going to make a door.

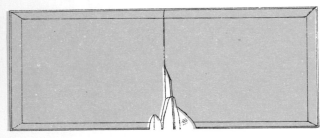

Score lightly across the lid.

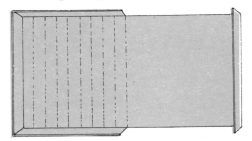

Mark out the other half of the lid into nine equal strips.

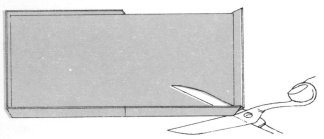

Cut away the top and bottom edges from one half.

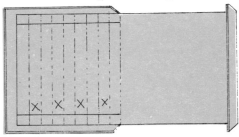

Mark every other strip. Make a border at the top and bottom.

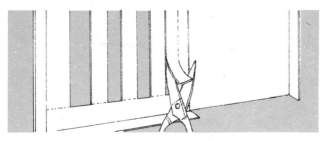

Cut out the cardboard from the marked strips only.

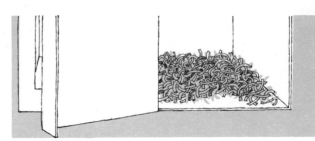

Use odd bits of wool for bedding inside the door.

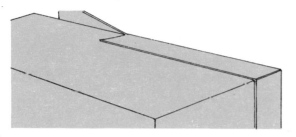

Stick the edges of the half of the lid that was cut into bars on to the main part of the box.

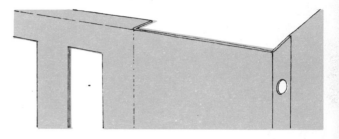

Use a paper fastener to fasten the door to the side of the box.

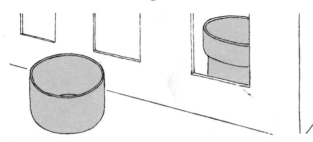

Put plastic containers for food and water in the barred end.

Put in the rabbits.

To make a chicken

Make a ball on two fingers as before, winding 30 times.

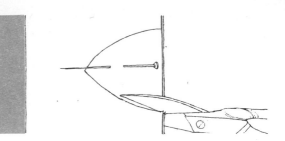

Pin the pattern on to a piece of felt and cut one out.

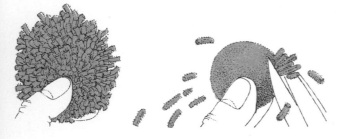

This time trim the ball quite small so that it is firm.

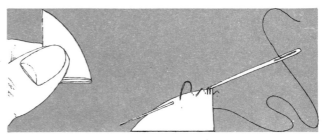

Fold the two corners of the beak together and stitch.

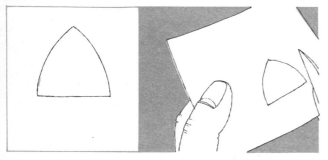

Trace the shape of the beak. Cut it out of paper.

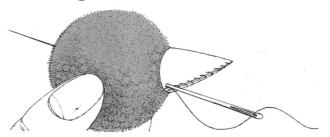

Stitch the beak into the head. Put the seam underneath and the point away from the head.

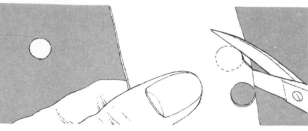

Cut out two small circles of felt for eyes.

Stitch the eyes through the center of the head on each side of the beak.

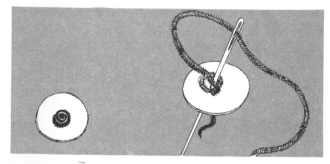

Make a black center by threading a wool knot through,

Trim a little more fluff away from the part around the eyes,

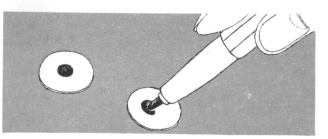

or by making a black mark with a felt tip pen.

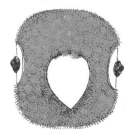

so that the head is a little flatter on the two sides.

The chicken can sit in an egg. Hard boil an egg: put it in cold water, bring to a boil. Cook it for 10 minutes.

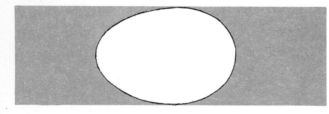

Leave it to get cold and dry.

Cover the egg with thin plastic. Tie it tightly at the top.

In the same way wrap the egg in white tissue paper over the plastic and tie at the top.

Spread glue over the tissue paper, not over the top bit.

Tear more tissue paper into small bits. Stick them all over the glue. Put on more glue and tissue paper, until there are at lea three even layers.

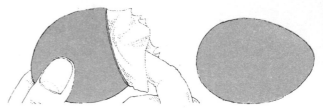

Now stick some layers of blue or brown tissue paper, or thicker white paper all over, overlapping the pieces. Finish by rubbing a little glue all over to make the surface smooth.

Take out the egg. Push back the plastic into the new egg shape.

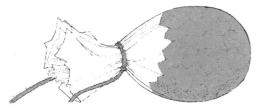

Leave it to dry well.

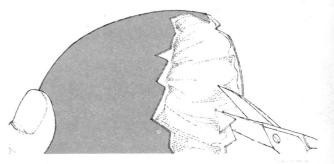

Cut the edge of the egg shape to look like broken egg shell. Flatten the bottom a little.

Cut away the top of the tissue and plastic.

Put the chicken into the egg.

 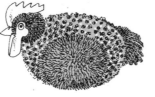

The chicken can have a mother hen. It is harder to make. A hand is too small to wind around for the body.

Slip off the wound wool.

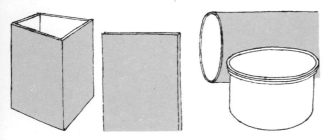

A box, a large tube or a wide piece of cardboard—even a wide jar or bottle will do.

Tie very tightly around the center. Cut through the loops.

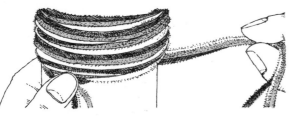

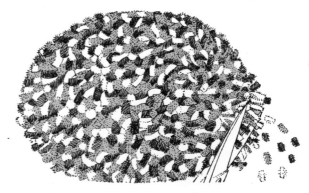

Wind four colors together 80 times, not too tightly.

Trim to a rough oval shape, but leave shaggy like feathers.

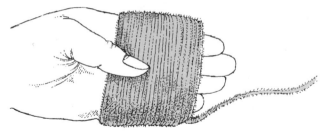

With plain wool and using four fingers, wind 60 times, to make a ball.

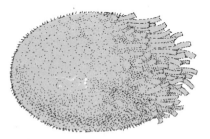

Do this twice. Trim these balls to an oval shape.

Then a third time, but this time leave one end of the oval shape untrimmed.

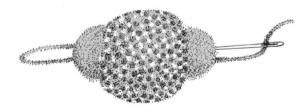

Stitch the two oval shapes to each flat side of the speckled wool. These are wings.

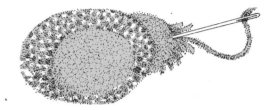

Now stitch the third oval to the long end of the body between the wings. The untrimmed edge facing away from the center makes the tail.

With the same plain colored wool, use two fingers and wind 30 times.

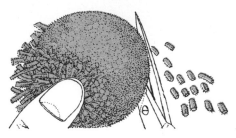

Trim this ball well so that
it is firm. This is the head.

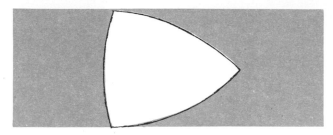

Cut a beak once from the
pattern in orange felt.

Cut a comb twice from the
pattern in felt.

Stitch the corners together
and stitch a pleat in the top.

Stick them together with clear
all-purpose glue.

Stitch the front of the comb
into the pleat of the beak.

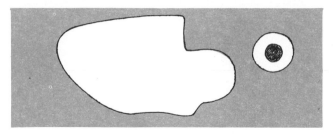

Cut two shapes for wattles
from the pattern.

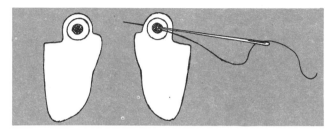

Cut two small circles for eyes,
give them black centers and
stitch them to the circular
part of each wattle.

Stitch a pleat in the wattle
below the eye.

Stitch the beak and the front
of the comb into the head. Let
the wool fluff around them.

On the same level as the beak
stitch through the two eyes,
well to the front of the head.
Stitch the head to the body.

Trim the hen to a good shape.

To make dolls

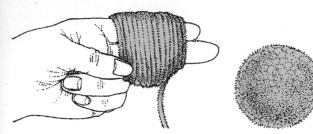

Make a head on two fingers, winding 30 times, and trim to a firm ball.

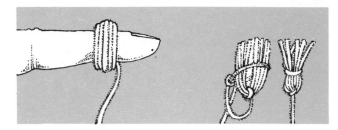

Or wind four times around one finger with white wool to make two tufts.

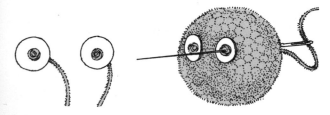

Make round eyes with a wool knot center. Stitch into head.

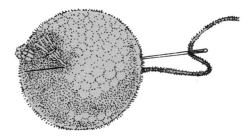

Stitch these into the head close together.

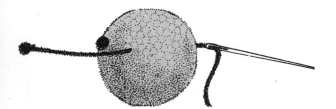

Or stitch two wool knots into the center of the head, leaving the knots on the surface of the ball.

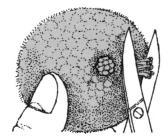

Trim them to the same length as the rest of the ball.

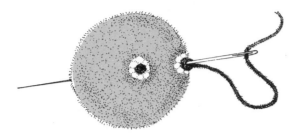

Then make a wool knot center.

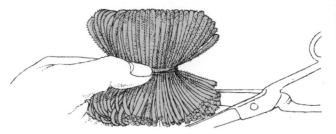

or cut only one end of the bundle, to make a skirt.

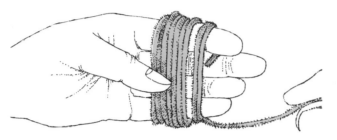

Make a body on four fingers, winding 60 times either in plain wool,

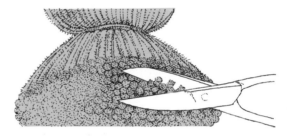

Trim these cut ends to make them as straight as possible.

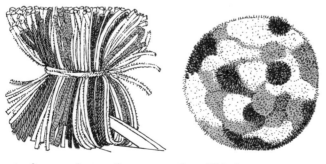

or in colored strands. Either cut and trim into a ball,

Braid three lengths of wool about 5 in. long.

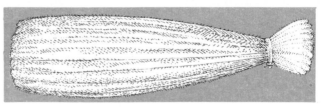

Tie the ends and leave a
tassel on each.

Slip off the hand and this
time tie in 2 places, once
about $\frac{3}{4}$ in. from the end.

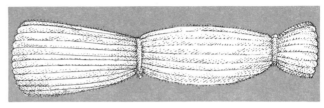

Tie the braid around the center
of the body.

And once about half way above
the first tie.

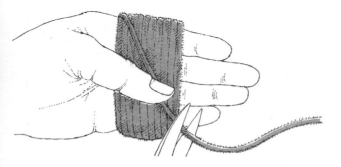

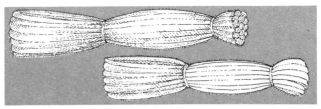

To make arms and legs, wind
15 times around four fingers.

Cut the end that was tied $\frac{3}{4}$ in.
from the edge unless you
want to join the dolls
together. If so, leave both
ends of the arms uncut.

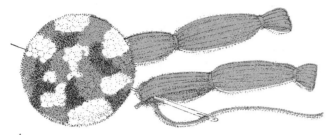 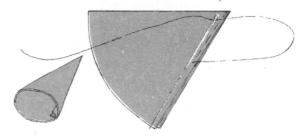

Stitch the legs to the bottom of the body, close together.

Join the straight edges and turn inside out.

 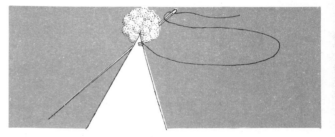

Stitch the arms and the head to the top half of the body.

Make a tiny woolly ball and stitch it in top of the hat.

 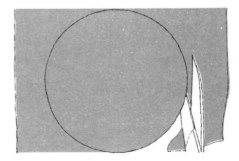

To make a hat, cut a piece of felt from the pattern.

Or cut hat brims from this pattern in felt.

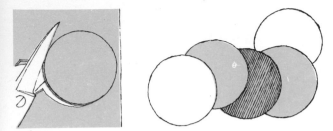

Cut five circles of felt from
this pattern, using three colors.
Put them on top of each other.

Thread them through the
centers of each circle and trim
to leave $1\frac{1}{4}$ in. of wool.

Stitch them to the center of
the brim.

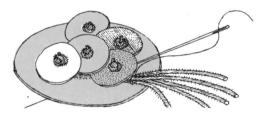

Stitch these flowers in the
center of the brim shape with
all the green wool together.

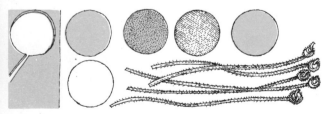

Or cut five smaller circles in
different colors. Make a knot
on the end of five pieces of
green wool.

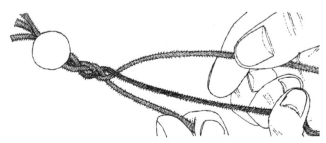

For hair braid three lengths of
wool 8 in. long.

Fluff out the ends beyond the knots with a needle.

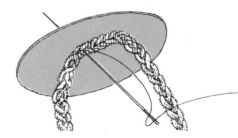

Stitch the braids to the center of the hat.

Tie a colored bow of wool just above each knot.

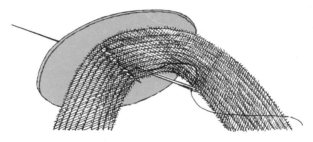

Stitch the hair to the underside of the hat.

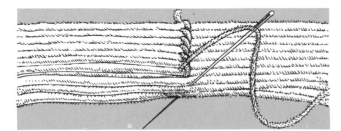

Or lay 10 lengths of wool 5 in. long side by side and stitch them together along the centers.

Stitch the flat hats firmly on to the top center of the heads.

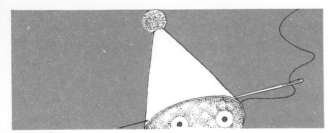

Stitch the pointed hat to the head at the two sides.

Join the dolls together in a row or a ring, by stitching the loops at the ends of their arms together.

Make a ring of dolls.

Make a row of dolls.

Or you can dangle the dolls on a string.

More ideas

Owl

Make one small and one large
ball—stitch together. Stitch
two large felt eyes on the front of
the small ball and two
wings cut from felt to the
sides of the big ball.
Stitch felt feet to the bottom.

Octopus

Make a very large ball and
four very long braids. Braid with
double wool to make it thicker.
Join the centers of the braids,
then stitch them into the
center of the ball.

Bee

Thread together a tiny, medium,
and large ball. Sew three lengths
of wool together at their
centers and join to center of
medium ball. Cut two net or
plastic wings and stitch to the top

sides of the medium ball.
Hang by wool between the wings.

Goldfish

Stitch a small and large ball
together, shaping them into an
oval. Stitch two big eyes to
each side of the small ball.
Stitch two felt fins to top and
bottom of large ball. Join the
centers of eight lengths of wool
together, stitching them to the
center of the large ball so
that they trail behind.

Elephant

Make a large ball for the body.
Stitch a medium ball to the
top and four tiny balls to one
side of the body.
Braid a trunk and stitch it to
the center of the head. Cut out
two felt ears and stitch to
sides of the head. Decorate a
plastic cup. Sit elephant on it.

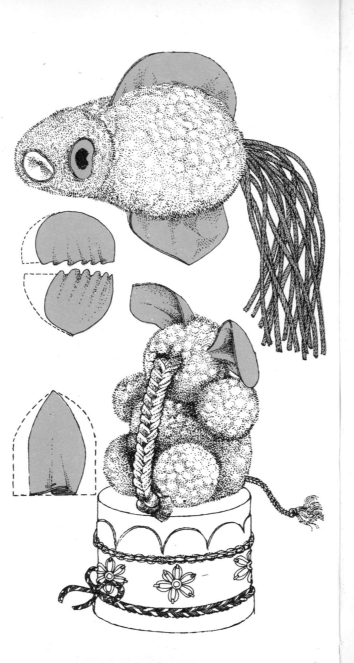

More ideas

Owl

Make one small and one large ball—stitch together. Stitch two large felt eyes on the front of the small ball and two wings cut from felt to the sides of the big ball. Stitch felt feet to the bottom.

Octopus

Make a very large ball and four very long braids. Braid with double wool to make it thicker. Join the centers of the braids, then stitch them into the center of the ball.

Bee

Thread together a tiny, medium, and large ball. Sew three lengths of wool together at their centers and join to center of medium ball. Cut two net or plastic wings and stitch to the top

sides of the medium ball.
Hang by wool between the wings.

Goldfish

Stitch a small and large ball
together, shaping them into an
oval. Stitch two big eyes to
each side of the small ball.
Stitch two felt fins to top and
bottom of large ball. Join the
centers of eight lengths of wool
together, stitching them to the
center of the large ball so
that they trail behind.

Elephant

Make a large ball for the body.
Stitch a medium ball to the
top and four tiny balls to one
side of the body.
Braid a trunk and stitch it to
the center of the head. Cut out
two felt ears and stitch to
sides of the head. Decorate a
plastic cup. Sit elephant on it.

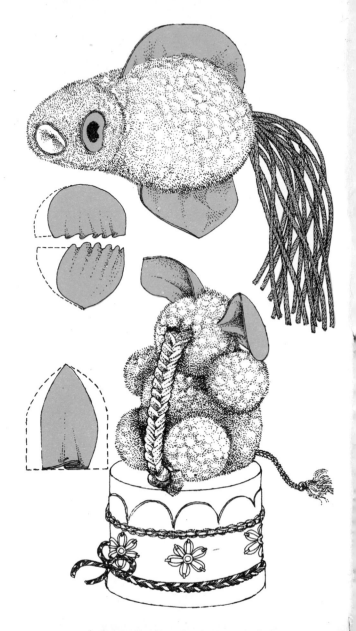